How to Draw
Illinois's
Sights and Symbols

Jenny Deinard

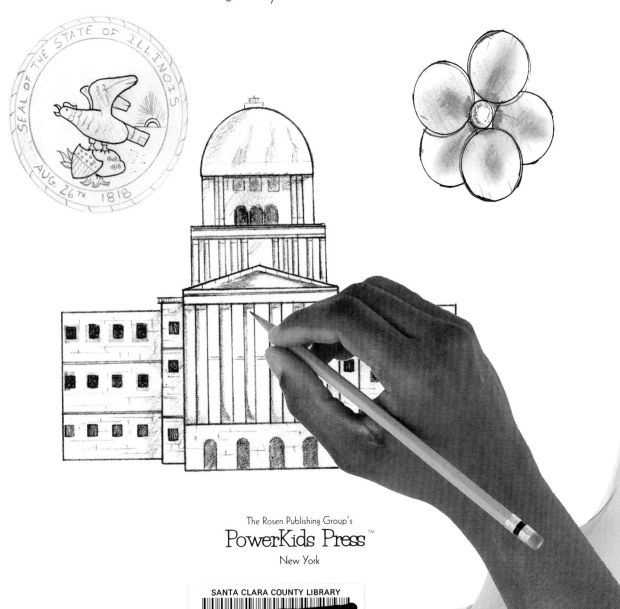

The Rosen Publishing Group's
PowerKids Press™
New York

Published in 2002 by The Rosen Publishing Group, Inc.
29 East 21st Street, New York, NY 10010

First Edition

Book Design: Kim Sonsky
Layout Design: Michael Donnellan
Project Editor: Jannell Khu

Illustration Credits: Jamie Grecco
Photo Credits: pp. 7, 16, 18, 20 © Index Stock; pp. 8 (photo and sketch), 9 (painting) © Brauer Museum of Art; pp. 12, 14 © One Mile Up, Incorporated; pp. 22, 26 © Richard Hamilton Smith/CORBIS; p. 24 © Bob Moore/SWI News.com; p. 28 © Roger Ressmeyer/CORBIS.

Deinard, Jenny.
How to draw Illinois's sights and symbols / Jenny Deinard.
p. cm. —(A kid's guide to drawing America)
Includes index.
Summary: This book describes how to draw some of Illinois's sights and symbols, including the state's seal, the state's flag, Fort de Chartres, and others.
  ISBN 0-8239-6069-2
1. Emblems, State—Illinois—Juvenile literature.   2. Illinois in art—Juvenile literature.   3. Drawing—Technique—Juvenile literature. [1. Emblems, State—Illinois.   2. Illinois.   3. Drawing—Technique] I. Title. II. Series.
  2001
  743'.8'09773—dc21

Manufactured in the United States of America

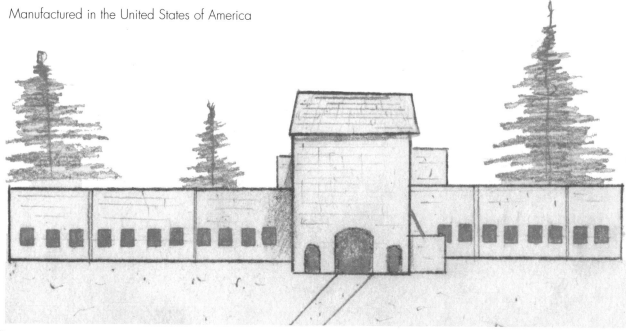

CONTENTS

1	Let's Draw Illinois	4
2	The Land of Lincoln	6
3	Artist in Illinois	8
4	Map of Illinois	10
5	The State Seal	12
6	The State Flag	14
7	The Violet	16
8	The White Oak	18
9	The Cardinal	20
10	The Illinois and Michigan Canal	22
11	Fort de Chartres	24
12	Illinois's Capitol	26
13	The Sears Tower	28
	Illinois State Facts	30
	Glossary	31
	Index	32
	Web Sites	32

Let's Draw Illinois

In 1673, two French explorers, Father Jacques Marquette and Louis Jolliet were the first Europeans to reach the area that would become Illinois. Almost 200 years later, on October 8, 1871, the Great Chicago Fire started in a barn. This fire ruined one-third of the city's buildings and killed 300 people.

Illinois is home to many industries. It is the country's biggest corn producer. Other businesses include industrial machinery, food processing, and motor vehicles. Illinois's Chicago is the largest city in the Midwest and the third-largest metropolitan area in the United States. Chicago boasts great museums like the Art Institute of Chicago, sports teams like basketball's Chicago Bulls and baseball's Chicago Cubs, and has incredible architecture, including famous skyscrapers like the Sears Tower.

You can learn how to draw many of Illinois's sights and symbols with this book. All of the drawings begin with a simple shape, and from there you will add other shapes. Under every drawing, directions explain how to do the step. Each new step of the drawing is shown in red to help guide you. Before you start, take a look at the drawing terms. These drawing terms show you the shapes and words used throughout this book. The last step of most of the drawings is to add shading. To shade, tilt your pencil to the side and hold it with your index finger. Now you are ready to learn about Illinois and to draw some of the state's sights and symbols. Have fun!

The supplies you will need to draw Illinois's sights and symbols are:

- A sketch pad
- An eraser
- A number 2 pencil
- A pencil sharpener

These are some of the shapes and drawing terms you need to know to draw Illinois's sights and symbols:

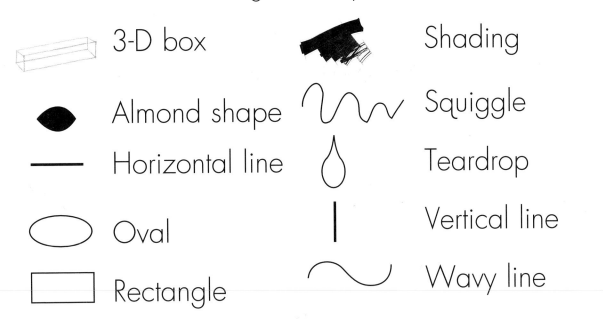

3-D box

Almond shape

Horizontal line

Oval

Rectangle

Shading

Squiggle

Teardrop

Vertical line

Wavy line

The Land of Lincoln

Illinois gets its name from a Native American tribe called the Illini, who lived in the region. Illinois was the twenty-first state to join the nation, on December 3, 1818. This Midwestern state covers 57,918 square miles (150,007 sq km), and is the twenty-fourth-largest state in the country. More than 12 million people live in Illinois, which makes it the sixth most populated state in the United States. The capital city is Springfield, with a population of 112,900. The most populated city is Chicago, which has nearly three million residents.

In 1955, Illinois accepted the Land of Lincoln as its nickname to honor Abraham Lincoln, who served as president from 1861 to 1865. Lincoln was born in Kentucky, but he lived most of his life in Illinois. As president Lincoln led the country through the Civil War, a war between the North and the South over issues such as slavery. Lincoln was killed by a man named John Wilkes Booth five days after the war ended.

President Abraham Lincoln wrote the Emancipation Proclamation, which freed all American slaves.

Artist in Illinois

Junius R. Sloan had no formal training as an artist, but he became one of the most well known painters of the Great Lakes region. Sloan was born in Kingsville, Ohio, in 1827. He taught himself to become a portrait painter. At the

Junius R. Sloan painted this self-portrait in 1858.

age of 21, Sloan left home to travel and paint in the Midwest. During his travels, he became a follower of the Hudson River school of art. This was a group of nineteenth-century American landscape painters whose work celebrated the beauty of natural scenery. Sloan

© Brauer Museum of Art

Junius R. Sloan used pencil and ink to create this 1855 sketch entitled *Log Cabin*.

loved spending time outdoors, especially in the summer months, during what he called the sketching season. He painted rural areas using clean, fresh lines. He worked in both oil and watercolors and his paintings showed the beauty of America's unspoiled land. Sloan believed in the Gospel of Beauty, which stated that landscape art was a way of representing the glory of God. He moved to Chicago in 1864, and he was one of that city's first resident landscape painters. In the late 1870s, Sloan was named vice president of the Chicago Academy of Design.

© Brauer Museum of Art

This is Junius R. Sloan's watercolor painting, *Road to the Lake—Rogers Park, Chicago*. It was painted in 1893 and measures 7 ⁵⁄₁₆ x 11 ¼ (18 cm x 28 cm).

Map of Illinois

Map of the Continental United States

Illinois borders the states of Wisconsin, Iowa, Indiana, Missouri, and Kentucky. The northeast corner of the state is on Lake Michigan, one of the five Great Lakes. Illinois has one national forest, the Shawnee National Forest. The state has many waterways, which include the Illinois, Ohio, and Mississippi Rivers. In fact, all of Illinois's western border is the Mississippi River. The Ohio River makes up almost half of the state's eastern border. The Upper Mississippi River National Wildlife and Fish Refuge is in the state's northwestern corner. The highest point in the state is Charles Mound, at 1,235 feet (376 m), and the lowest point is the Mississippi River, at 279 feet (85 m).

1

Draw a rectangle.

2

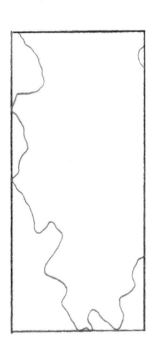

Using the rectangle as a guide, draw the shape of Illinois.

3

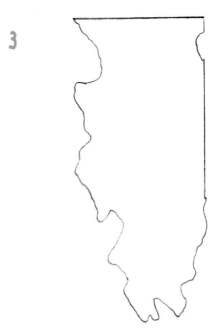

Erase extra lines.

4

☆	Springfield
▯	Sears Tower
○	Adler Planetarium
//	Canal locks
⬜	Fort de Chartres

a. Draw a rectangle to mark the Sears Tower.
b. Draw in the canal locks by using two bent lines.
c. Use a circle to draw the Adler Planetarium.
d. Use two squares to draw Fort de Chartres.
e. Draw a star to mark Illinois's capital, Springfield.

11

The State Seal

Illinois has had five state seals since 1788, all of which have had an image of a bald eagle. Since 1868, the seal has remained basically unchanged. The bald eagle is a symbol of America and of strength. The sun rising on the horizon behind the eagle represents hope and the future. The rock on which the eagle stands is in a prairie, for which Illinois is famous. In its beak, the eagle holds a banner that shows the state's motto, "State Sovereignty, National Union." The two dates on the rock are the year the present state seal was designed, 1868, and the year Illinois became a state, 1818. The date on the bottom of the seal, August 26, 1818, is the date that the first Illinois constitution was signed in Kaskaskia, Illinois.

1

Draw three circles, one inside the other.

2

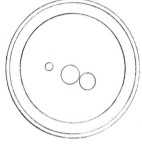

Add three circles, as shown, to form the eagle's head and body.

3

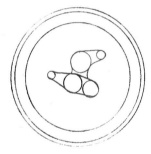

Connect the circles. Add two more circles to make the eagle's wing. Connect these circles, too.

4

Erase any extra lines. Add a beak, feet, and a tail.

5

Use a triangle to draw the shield.

6

Draw a rock under the eagle's feet. Draw two half circles for the sun in the background.

7

Start working on the border by drawing slanted lines.

8

Use triangles to make the leaves beneath the shield. Add as much detail as you'd like to finish your seal.

The State Flag

Illinois has had two official state flags. On July 6, 1915, Illinois adopted a flag designed by Lucy Derwent from Rockford, Illinois. The Illinois state flag is white with the image from the state seal in the center. Until 1969, the word "Illinois" was not written under the image of the seal. Chief Petty Officer Bruce McDaniel of Illinois was serving in the Vietnam War when, one day, he noticed that the state flag did not bear the state's name. He requested that the state alter the flag. On September 17, 1969, the General Assembly authorized that "Illinois" be written in blue block letters under the image on the state flag.

1

Draw a rectangle for the background.

2

Add three circles to form the eagle's head and body.

3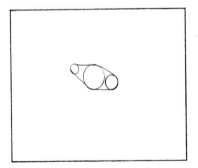

Connect the circles.

4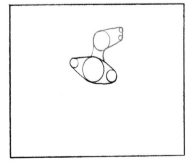

Add three more circles for the eagle's wing. Connect them, too.

5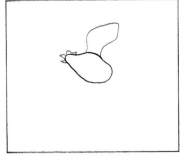

Erase extra lines. Add a beak and head feathers to the eagle.

6

Use rectangles to draw the eagle's legs and tail. Draw in its feet. Use a wavy line to form the rock.

7

Draw the eagle's second wing. Use a triangle to draw the shield.

8

Erase any extra lines and smudges. Write "ILLINOIS" at the flag's bottom. Add detail, such as more feathers on the eagle.

15

The Violet

The violet was chosen as Illinois's state flower in 1908. Violets come not only in the color violet, but also in yellow or white. There are at least 30 species of violets in Illinois. Violets are small flowers about 1 inch (3 cm) wide with five petals. Violets can usually be seen between March and June. They grow in all of Illinois's 102 counties, in a variety of habitats including prairies, forests, and wetlands. Violets are a common diet for rabbits, and the seeds of violets are eaten by mice and by many birds. People eat violets, too. In fact, violets contain vitamins A and C. The flowers are especially nutritious tossed in salads. Coated with sugar, violets make beautiful, edible cake decorations!

1

Draw a circle for the center of the flower.

2

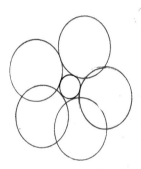

Add five circles around the center. It's okay if the circles overlap.

3

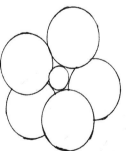

Erase any extra lines.

4

Draw straight lines in the center of the petals.

5

Add shading and detail to your flower. Erase extra smudges and your violet is complete.

The White Oak

The oak became Illinois's state tree in 1908. There are 18 species of oak trees in Illinois, so the state tree was narrowed down to the white oak in 1973. White oaks can reach 100 feet (30.5 m) in height, can grow to 3 feet (91 cm) in diameter, and can live as long as 350 to 400 years! An oak tree's trunk is covered with a light gray, scaly bark. The leaves are bright green, and each leaf has seven to nine round lobes. Oak trees carry acorn seeds that are eaten by deer, squirrels, wild turkeys, and other animals. Colonists used oak wood to make houses, and they fed their pigs acorns from oak trees. People still use oak today to make objects like furniture.

Draw a rectangle.

Draw branches using wavy lines. The more branches you draw, the more full your tree will look.

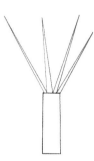

Draw thin triangles above the rectangle.

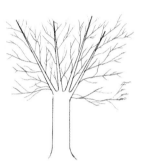

Add leaves. You can draw the leaves by making little M's.

Erase extra lines at the top and bottom of the rectangle.

Add shading and detail to your tree. Erase any extra smudges.

The Cardinal

The cardinal (*Cardinalis cardinalis*) was chosen as Illinois's state bird in 1929. Male and female cardinals have different coloring. Male cardinals are bright red with black around their eyes and beak. Female cardinals are pale brown with soft red highlights. Both cardinals have crests on their heads. Both male and female cardinals are between 7½ to 8 inches (19–20 cm) long, including a 4-inch (10-cm) tail. Cardinals build their nests in bushes and shrubs about 1 yard (1 m) off the ground, and they don't mind being near humans. Cardinals eat insects, grain, wild fruit, and seeds, especially sunflower seeds. Female cardinals lay three or four bluish white eggs that have small, brown dots. Cardinals' songs sound cheerful and their trills usually last for about 3 seconds.

1

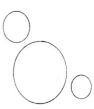

Draw three circles for the bird's head and body.

2

Connect the circles.

3

Erase any extra lines.

4

Draw one triangle for the beak, one for the wing, and one for the plume on top of the bird's head.

5

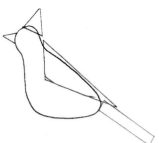

Draw the shape of the wing as shown. Draw a rectangle for the tail.

6

Erase any extra lines. Draw the eye.

7

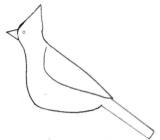

Draw four thin lines to make the bird's legs. Draw six lines for the feet.

8

Add detail and shading. You can use your finger to smudge the pencil lines.

21

The Illinois and Michigan Canal

On July 4, 1836, ground was broken to begin a canal that would connect the Illinois River to Lake Michigan. The canal was completed in 1848. In April 1848, the first canal barge, pulled by mules on the towpath, made the 97-mile (156-km) journey from La Salle, Illinois, to Lake Michigan. The creation of the canal turned Chicago into a major port. In 1850, only 30,000 people lived in Chicago. By 1870, that number had grown to 299,000! Along the canal are canal locks, or limestone locks, which control the water level in the canal. These locks raise and lower boats, allowing them to travel on the river.

1

Draw a long line and a short line as shown.

2

Connect the two lines to form a slanted rectangle.

3

Draw another long line and another short line as shown.

4

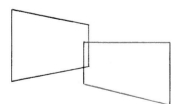

Connect the lines to form another slanted rectangle. This is the shape of the canal's walls.

5

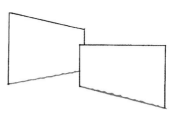

Erase extra lines.

6

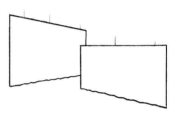

Add short lines above the canal to make the tree trunks.

7

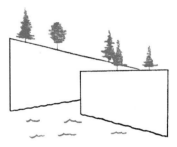

Extend the long wall. Use the side of your pencil to shade in the trees. You can also add wavy lines in the water.

8

Add shading and detail to the canal. Add rectangles to form the stones in the walls. Erase any smudges.

23

Fort de Chartres

An eighteenth-century fort named Fort de Chartres stands near Prairie du Rocher, Illinois, on the banks of the Mississippi River. The fort was built by the French colonial government in 1720. At the time Fort de Chartres was built, France owned Illinois territory. In 1763, Great Britain gained the land from the French as part of a treaty made after the French and Indian War. In 1765, British troops took over the fort and renamed it Fort Cavendish. The British abandoned the fort in 1772, and it fell to ruin. In 1913, the fort's site became a state park. Today Fort de Chartres has been partially rebuilt to show what it once looked like under French rule.

1

Draw a rectangle.

2

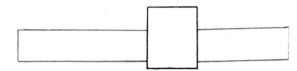

Draw two long rectangles.

3

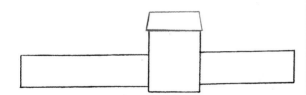

Add a rectangle with two slanted lines. This is the fort's roof.

4

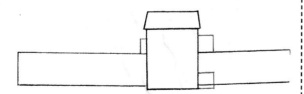

Draw three small rectangles as shown.

5

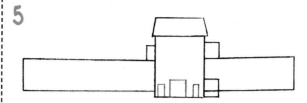

Add three thin rectangles for doors.

6

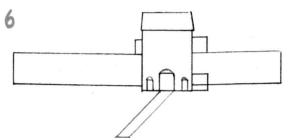

Round the top of the doors. Add a long rectangle for the road.

7

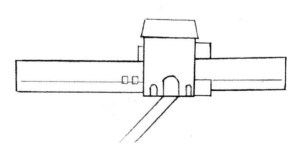

Draw a thin line across the building as a guide for your windows. Add the windows.

8

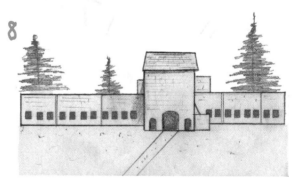

Add shading and detail to your building. You can also add triangle shapes to form trees. Erase any extra smudges.

Illinois's Capitol

The Illinois state capitol building is in Springfield, the state's capital city. The building seen today is the state's sixth capitol, which was built between 1868 and 1888. Its 361-foot-high (110-m-high) dome is 74 feet (22.5 m) taller than the dome on the U.S. Capitol Building in Washington, D.C. The old state capitol, which served as the state's capitol from 1839 to 1876, is the most famous of all the state capitol buildings because it is where Abraham Lincoln worked. When Lincoln worked there during the 1840s and 1850s, the building was the center of the capital city's cultural life. Concerts, speeches, dances, rallies, and conventions took place both inside and outside this great building.

1

Draw three rectangles to form the front of the capitol building.

2

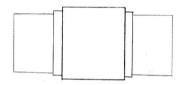

Add a rectangle on either side as shown.

3

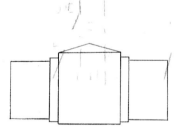

Draw a triangle on top of the center rectangle.

4

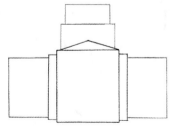

Add two rectangles to form the base of the building's dome.

5

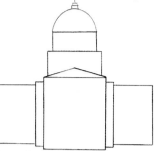

Add a half circle for the dome. Add two tiny rectangles to form the dome's peak.

6

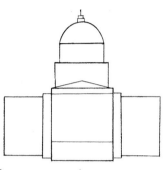

Draw two lines across the center rectangle.

7

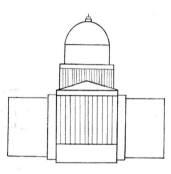

Add columns to the building using thin rectangles.

8

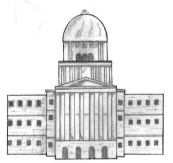

Add shading and detail to your building. You can form windows by drawing squares as shown. Erase any extra smudges.

27

The Sears Tower

The Sears Tower was more than 1,700 feet (518 m) tall when it was completed in 1973. This made it the world's largest building at the time. The Sears Tower is located in Chicago and was designed by architect Bruce Graham for Sears, Roebuck and Company. The Sears Tower covers two city blocks and has 101 acres (41 ha) of space within it. It has bronze-tinted glass windows and a stainless aluminum exterior. The roofline rises ¼ mile (.4 km), or 1,454 feet (443 m) above the ground. The building has 110 floors, and its highest occupied floor is 1,431 feet (436 m) off the ground. The tower has more than 16,000 windows and 16 double-decker elevators.

1

Draw a long, straight line. This is the center of the tower.

2

Draw a small, slanted rectangle.

3

Add a long rectangle and a short rectangle.

4

Draw three slanted rectangles as shown.

5

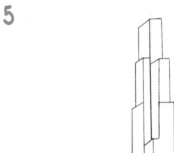

Add four more rectangles.

6

Add shading to the tower, and draw two antennas on the roof of the building. You can use the side of your pencil to draw clouds.

Illinois State Facts

Statehood	December 3, 1818, 21st state
Area	57,918 square miles (150,007 sq km)
Population	12,128,400
Capital	Springfield, population, 112,900
Most Populated City	Chicago, population, 2,768,500
Industries	Industrial machinery, food processing, chemicals, metals, rubber, plastic
Agriculture	Corn, soybeans, hogs, cattle, dairy products
Tree	White oak
Bird	Cardinal
Flower	Violet
Animal	White-tailed deer
Dance	Square dance
Fish	Bluegill
Fossil	Tully monster (soft-bodied marine animal)
Insect	Monarch butterfly
Mineral	Fluorite
Motto	State Sovereignty, National Union
Nicknames	The Land of Lincoln, the Prairie State, the Corn State
Grass	Big bluestem
Slogan	Land of Lincoln

Glossary

adopted (uh-DOPT-ed) To have accepted ot approved something.

architecture (AR-kih-tek-chur) The science, art, or profession of designing buildings.

constitution (kahn-stih-TOO-shun) The basic rules used to govern a state or country.

conventions (kun-VEN-shunz) A formal meeting for some special purpose.

cultural (KUL-chuh-ruhl) Having to do with the beliefs, customs, art, and religions of a group of people.

diameter (dy-A-meh-tur) The distance across the center of an object.

habitats (HA-bih-tats) Surroundings where an animal or plant naturally lives.

lobes (LOHBZ) Curved or rounded divisions or projections.

locks (LAHX) Areas in canals with closures at both ends that allow water to rise and fall so that a boat can move from one level to another.

metropolitan (meh-truh-PAH-lih-ten) Having to do with a large city.

moat (MOHT) A deep, wide ditch that surrounds a castle or town for protection against an enemy.

nutritious (noo-TRIH-shus) Useful as a food.

portrait (POHR-treht) A picture, often a painting, of a known person.

prairie (PRAIR-ee) Grassland.

refuge (REH-fyooj) A place that gives shelter or protection.

scaly (SKAY-lee) Covered with small flakes.

sovereignty (SAHV-er-in-tee) Freedom from outside control.

species (SPEE-sheez) A single kind of plant or animal.

towpath (TOH-path) A path along a canal that allows animals to help tow boats.

trills (TRILZ) Birdsong.

Vietnam War (vee-eht-NAHM WOR) A war fought between South Vietnam and North Vietnam from the late 1960s to the early 1970s, in which America was involved.

Index

C
canal locks, 22
capitol, 26
Civil War, 6
corn, 4

D
Derwent, Lucy, 14

F
food processing, 4
Fort de Chartres, 24

G
Great Chicago Fire, 4

J
Jolliet, Louis, 4

L
Lincoln, President
    Abraham, 6, 26

M
Marquette, Father
    Jacques, 4
McDaniel, Chief Petty
    Officer Bruce, 14
Mississippi River, 10,
    24
motor vehicles, 4

O
old state capitol, 26

S
Sears Tower, 4, 28
Sloan, Junius R., 8, 9

Springfield, Illinois, 6,
    26
state bird, 20
state flag, 14
state flower, 16
state seal, 12

T
towpath, 22

V
Vietnam War, 14

W
White Oak, 18

Web Sites

To learn more about Illinois, check out this Web site:
www.state.il.us